The B-52 Story

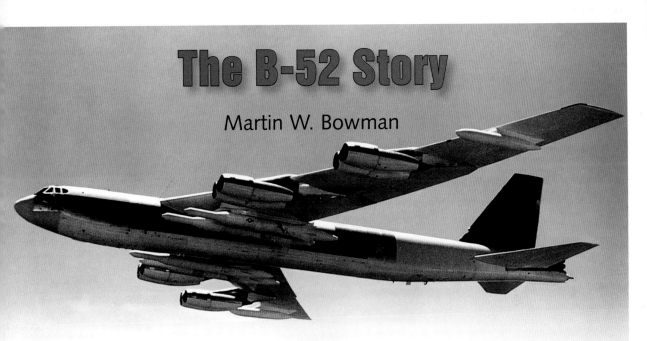

The B-52 Story

Martin W. Bowman

The
HISTORY
Press

Published in the United Kingdom in 2012 by
The History Press
The Mill · Brimscombe Port · Stroud · Gloucestershire
GL5 2QG

Martin W. Bowman has asserted his moral right to be
identified as the author of this work.

British Library Cataloguing in Publication Data
A catalogue record for this book is available from the
British Library.

Hardback ISBN 978-0-7524-8282-8

Typesetting and origination by The History Press
Printed in India

'Fighter pilots make movies – bombers make history'

Half-title page: B-52G being refuelled air-to-air from a KC-135 in 1984. (USAF)
Title verso: B-52D being air-to-air refuelled. (USAF)
Title page: B-52H armed with Douglas GAM-87A Skybolt Air Launched Ballistic Missiles (ALBMs).
➤ B-52G 57-6498 carrying a Boeing AGM-86B Air Launched Cruise Missile (ALCM) in formation
with F-4 Phantoms.

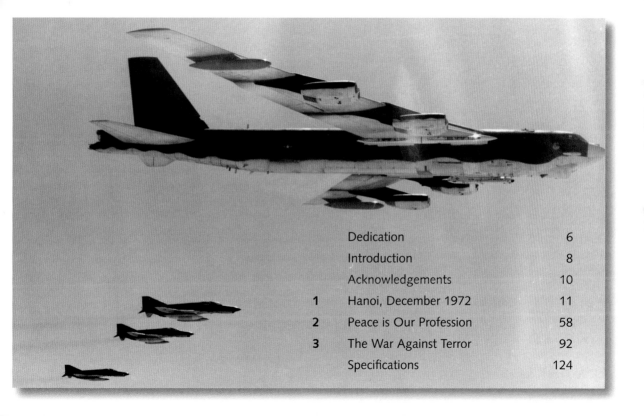

SOUTH VIETNAM: ĐỖ VĂN VŨ, HUỲNH THÀNH MỸ, NGUYỄN MẪN HIẾU, VŨ VĂN GIANG, **NORTH VIETNAM**: BÙI ĐÌNH TÙY, ĐẶNG VĂN HẰNG, ĐINH ĐỆ, ĐỖ VĂN NHÂN, ĐOÀN PHI HÙNG, DƯƠNG CÔNG THIÊN, DƯƠNG THÀNH VĂN, HỒ CA, HỒ VĂN ĐỆ, HỒ VĂN TƯ, HOÀNG TƯ, HOÀNG CHÂU, HUỲNH VĂN DŨNG, HUỲNH VĂN HƯỚNG, HUỲNH VĂN HỮU, HUỲNH VĂN TRÍ, KIM VĂN TƯỚC, LÊ ĐÌNH DƯ, LÊ KHẮC TÂM, LÊ KIA, LÊ THỊ NẮNG, LƯƠNG NGHĨA DŨNG, LƯƠNG TÁN ĐỨC, LÝ VĂN CAO, NGỌC HƯƠNG, NGỌC NHU, NGUYỄN ĐỨC THÀNH, NGUYỄN DŨNG, NGUYỄN HƯƠNG NĂM, NGUYỄN HUY, NGUYỄN LƯƠNG NAM, NGUYỄN NGỌC TÚ, NGUYỄN NHẤT HOA, NGUYỄN OANH LIỆT, NGUYỄN THANH HIỀN, NGUYỄN TRUNG ĐỊNH, NGUYỄN VĂN CHIẾN 1, NGUYỄN VĂN CHIẾN 2, NGUYỄN VĂN HƯƠNG, NGUYỄN VĂN MẪN, NGUYỄN VĂN NĂNG, NGUYỄN VĂN NHU, NGUYỄN VĂN THA, NGUYỄN VĂN THẮNG, NGUYỄN VĂN THUẬN, NGUYỄN VĂN THUÝ, NGUYỄN VĂN UNG, NGUYỄN VIỆT HIỀN, PHẠM CỔ PHÁC, PHẠM TRANH, PHẠM VĂN KHƯƠNG, PHẠM VŨ BÌNH, PHÙNG QUANG LIÊM, SÁU VĂN, THANH THỊNH, THÔI HỮU, TÔ ĐỊNH, TRẦN ĐÌNH KHUÔL, TRẦN NGỌC ĐĂNG, TRẦN OAI DŨNG, TRẦN XUÂN HY, TRỊNH ĐÌNH HY, TRƯƠNG PHÚ THIÊN, VÕ ĐỨC HIỆP, VÕ NGỌC KHANH, VÕ VĂN LƯƠNG, VÕ VĂN QUÝ, VŨ HANH, VŨ HÙNG DŨNG, VŨ NGỌC TÔNG.

This book is dedicated to the memory of Buck Rigg and to the war photographers displayed on these tablets in the War Remnants Museum in Saigon. (Author)

Dickey Chapelle (Georgette Louise Meyer) always arranged to be in the field with her beloved marines, parachuted with them several times into the thick of the fighting and was killed by shrapnel from a land mine near Da Nang in November 1965. She was 46 and remains the only American war correspondent killed in action.

The day he died, Ollie Noonan Jr got exclusive pictures of fierce fighting, then put aside his cameras to help carry the wounded. He was rushing to get his film to Da Nang when his helicopter was shot down. His cameras were later recovered and the film was still intact. Noonan was laid to rest in the family burial plot on Campobello Island. His friends at the *Boston Globe* added this poem he had sent from Vietnam to the newspaper's obituary:

ON THE SIDE THAT'S WINNING

THE MOON HANGS LIKE A TEAR

AND I, SENSING IMMORTALITY

BUT AFRAID OF TOMORROW, RUSH TO GREET IT

AFRAID TO DIE

AND KEEP RUNNING,

AFRAID TO REALIZE IT MAY BE HOPELESS

TO CARRY TEARS ON MY SLEEVE

WHILE RIGHT BEHIND ME, IN CLOAK AND GOWN

THE MAN'S JUGGLING BOMBS

LIKE A CIRCUS CLOWN

THOUGH THE BELLS TOLL

THEY CAN BOMB THE LAND

BUT NOT THE SOUL.

AUSTRALIA: ALAN HIRONS, **AUSTRIA**: GEORG GENSLUCKNER, BRITAIN LARRY BURROWS, JAMES GILL. **THE CAMBODIANS**: CHEA HO, CHHIM SARATH, CHHOR VUTHI, HENG HO, KIM SA VATH, KOUY SARUN, LANH DAUNH RAR, LEK, LENG, LY ENG, LYNG NHAN, PEN, PUT SOPHAN, SAING HEL, SOU VICHITH, SUN HEANG, THONG VEASNA, TY MANY, VANTHA. **GERMANY**: DIETER BELLENDORF. **UNITED SATATES**: ROBERT CAPA, SAM CASTAN, DICKEY CHAPELLE, CHARLES RICHARD EGGLESTON, ROBERT J. ELLISION, SEAN FLYNN, RONALD D. GALLAGHER. NEIL K. HULBERT. BERNARD KOLENBERG, OLIVER E. NOONAN, KENT POTTER, EVERETTE DIXIE REESE, TERRY REYNOLDS, JERRY A. ROSE, DANA STONE, PETER RONARD VAN THIEL. **FRANCE**: CLAUDE ARPIN-PONT, FRANCIS BAILLY, GILLES CARON, FRANZ DALMA, BERNARD B. FALL. GERARD HEBERT, HENRI HUET, PIERRE ANDRE JAHAN, MICHEL LAURENT, RAYMOND MARTINOFF, JEAN PERAUD, FRANCOIS SULLY. **JAPAN**: TAIZO ICHINOSE, HIROMICHI MINE, KEIZABURO SHIMAMOTO, KYOICHI SAWADA. **SINGAPORE**: CHARLES CHELLAPPAH, TERRENCE KHOO, SAM KAI FAYE. **SWITZERLAND**: WILLY METTLER.

Incredibly, development of the Boeing B-52 global bomber was begun in June 1945, the first of these remarkable aircraft flew on 15 April 1952 and they are still in service today. Always ready at a moment's notice, the B-52 has been in continuous operational service since the huge bomber was introduced in 1957, first with SAC

(Strategic Air Command) as a high-level nuclear bomber, and later with ACC (Air Combat Command) and the Air Force Reserve. The B-52, or High Altitude Plough or Aluminum Overcast, came to symbolise America's nuclear defence posture in the Cold War with the Soviet Bloc, which rapidly became one of Mutually Assured Destruction (MAD). Also known as the 'Buff', the B-52 has been much modified and upgraded on many occasions and has been used in several new roles, including service as a low-level strike aircraft and delivery platform for air-launched cruise missiles since it was originally conceived as the mainstay of the USAF's strategic nuclear force. It is anticipated that the B-52 will continue to serve as a first-line aircraft until 2040. Apart from the formidable deterrent it provided during the Cold War, the Stratofortress has fulfilled vital roles in all US overseas military operations in South-East Asia, through to the brief Desert Storm campaign in 1991, the Balkan conflict, Afghanistan and the liberation of Iraq. Some 744 examples were built; the last during 1959–62, when thirty-nine B-52Gs and 102 B-52Hs brought production to an end. Today, around eighty remain in service.

ACKNOWLEDGEMENTS

Thanks to: Technical Sergeant Shawn M. Bohannon, 2nd Bomb Wing Historian; Roger Chesneau; DAVA; Peter E. Davies; Jessica D'Aurizio, 917th Wing, Air Force Reserve Command Public Affairs; Lieutenant Jesse Hildebrand USAF; Lieutenant Jim Ivie, 2nd Bomb Wing Public Affairs; Lieutenant-Colonel Steve Kirkpatrick; Technical Sergeant Barbara Lavigne, 2nd Bomb Wing Public Affairs; Frank B. Mormillo; Bob Ogden; H.D. 'Buck' Rigg, Historian, Barksdale AFB; Jerry Scutts; Anthony Thornborough; Tracey Woods.

Lieutenant-Colonel Don L. Rissi was not best pleased. The B-52G pilot and aircraft commander from the 97th Bomb Wing based at Blytheville AFB, Arkansas, had finished his tour of TDY, or temporary duty, at Andersen Air Force Base on Guam, the largest of the Marianas Islands in the West Pacific, 2,600 miles from Saigon. He was preparing to go home but a frustrating delay in replacing him meant that he would not be home for Christmas 1972 after all. An aura of invincibility seemed to pervade B-52 operations although some questions had been raised in April during the so-called 'special missions' over the North. At Guam that summer everyone was told that the Vietnam War was almost over. Probably they would not fly the required twenty missions to qualify for an Air Medal. Then, each month, regular as clockwork, there was the 15th of the month rumour that the G models were going home. Every month, that is, until December – then there was an aircraft commanders' meeting. For over a day, all bombing missions in Vietnam had been cancelled. The rumours really started flying: 'War with China', 'War with Russia', 'G models

▼ The remains of *Charcoal 1* at the Bảo Tàng Chilến Thầng B-52 Museum in Hanoi. (Author)

going home', 'Everyone going home'. But, like the dramatic scene in *Twelve O'Clock High* when Gregory Peck tells the bomber crews that they aren't going home, 'they are going to die', and they should consider themselves 'already

Did you know?
In Vietnam the first Arc Light mission, as the B-52 operations were known, took place on 18 June 1965.

➤ Two of the engines from *Charcoal 1*. (Author)

dead', the odds suddenly did not look good for Rissi or the others. On 7 November Richard M. Nixon had won a massive presidential re-election victory and he was determined to end the long-drawn-out war in Vietnam, even if it meant using them to bomb the North Vietnamese capital, Hanoi, to destruction. When Rissi and the other aircraft commanders returned from the aircraft commanders' meeting, all they could tell their crews was that they should order two lunches and get lots of sleep.

During the Cold War, the fleet of B-52s were at a moment's readiness to make a one-way trip to targets in the Soviet Union,

and initially, SAC had argued that dropping conventional bombs in Vietnam was not their 'business'. The first ARC LIGHT mission, as the B-52 operations were known, finally took place on 18 June 1965 when twenty-seven B-52Fs loaded with 750lb and 1,000lb bombs took off from Guam to bomb a suspected Viet Cong strongpoint in the Bên Cat Special Zone, 40 miles north-west of Saigon. Two of the B-52s were involved in a mid-air collision over the South China Sea while refuelling en route to the target. Eight of the twelve aircrew were killed. As early as 1968, during a visit to Air Defence HQ, Ho Chi Minh had predicted that the B-52s would come to Hanoi one day. Finally, on 30 November 1972 President Richard M. Nixon signalled his intentions to bomb Hanoi with B-52s, dismissing fears of losses. On Guam there were 150 B-52D and B-52G crews of the 72nd Strategic Wing (P) and another sixty B-52D crews at U-Tapao in Thailand. On 3 December the mayor of Hanoi began to evacuate civilians from the city. On 6 December Nixon ordered the Joint Chiefs of Staff to begin planning for strikes 'as close as can reasonably be risked' that would 'create the most massive

◄◄ *Cobalt 1*, which was shot down on the night of 27/28 December 1972. The wreckage of a B-52G lies in the community pond at Ngoc Hi, North Vietnam. During the LINEBACKER II campaign, 729 B-52 sorties were flown at a cost of fifteen B-52s (nine B-52Ds and six B-52Gs) that were all hit by SAMs. (USN)

◄ The remains of *Cobalt 1* in the same location, thirty-eight years later. (Author)

DI TÍCH LỊCH SỬ

HỒ HỮU TIẾP VÀ XÁC MÁY BAY B52

PHƯỜNG NGỌC HÀ - QUẬN BA ĐÌNH - HÀ NỘI

HỒI 23 GIỜ 05 PHÚT NGÀY 27 THÁNG 12 NĂM 1972, TIỂU ĐOÀN 72 - TRUNG ĐOÀN 285 TÊN LỬA PHÒNG KHÔNG ĐÃ BẮN RƠI TẠI CHỖ 1 MÁY BAY B52G CỦA ĐẾ QUỐC MỸ XÂM PHẠM VÙNG TRỜI HÀ NỘI. MỘT PHẦN XÁC MÁY BAY RƠI XUỐNG HỒ HỮU TIẾP - PHƯỜNG NGỌC HÀ, QUẬN BA ĐÌNH, HÀ NỘI.

CHIẾN CÔNG XUẤT SẮC NÀY ĐÃ GÓP PHẦN LÀM NÊN CHIẾN THẮNG "ĐIỆN BIÊN PHỦ TRÊN KHÔNG": ĐÁNH BẠI CUỘC TẬP KÍCH CHIẾN LƯỢC BẰNG MÁY BAY B52 CỦA ĐẾ QUỐC MỸ VÀO HÀ NỘI CUỐI ... 12 NĂM 1972, TẠO BƯỚC CHUYỂN QUAN TRỌNG ... A SỰ NGHIỆP CHỐNG MỸ CỨU NƯỚC CỦA ... ÂN TỘC VIỆT NAM ĐẾN THẮNG LỢI HOÀN TOÀN.

HISTORICAL VESTIGE

HUU TIEP LAKE AND THE WRECKAGE OF B52 BOMBE

NGOC HA PRECINCT - BA DINH DISTRICT - HA NOI

AT 23.05 ON DECEMBER 27TH 1972, TH BATTALION No 72 - AIR DEFENCE MISSIL REGIMENT No 285 SHOT DOWN ON THE SPOT B52G OF THE US IMPERIALIST VIOLATING HA N AIR SPACE. A PART OF THE WRECKAGE FELL IN T HUU TIEP LAKE - NGOC HA PRECINCT, BA DIN DISTRICT, HA NOI.

THE OUTSTANDING FEAT OF ARM CONTRIBUTE TO ACHIEVING THE VICTORY "DIEN BIEN PHU I THE AIR": DEFEATING THE US IMPERIALIST STRATEGIC AIR RAID WITH B52 BOMBER AGAINS HA NOI AT THE END OF DECEMBER 1972 AN CREATING AN IMPORTANT CHANGE THAT LED TH VIETNAMESE PEOPLE'S ANTI-US RESISTANCE FO NATIONAL SALVATION TO THE COMPLET VICTORY.

shock effect in a psychological context'. On 13 December the North Vietnamese walked out of the Paris peace talks and the next day Nixon ordered the LINEBACKER II bombing campaign against Hanoi to begin on Sunday 17 December.

The LINEBACKER B-52 operations were the responsibility of General John C. Meyer, the chief of Strategic Air Command (SAC) at his Headquarters at Offutt AFB, Omaha, Nebraska. After approval by the Joint Chiefs of Staff the plans were sent to Lieutenant-General Gerald W. Johnson commanding the 8th Air Force at Andersen AFB and General John W. Voght commanding 7th Air Force in Saigon. Meyer, Johnson and Voght had been among the highest scoring fighter pilots in England during the Second World War.

On 17 December the 7th and 8th Air Force commanders were directed by the JCS 'to commence at approximately 1200Z, 18 December 1972 a three-day maximum effort, repeat maximum effort, of B-52/Tacair strikes in the Hanoi/Haiphong areas against the targets contained in the authorised target list. Object is maximum destruction of selected military targets in the vicinity of Hanoi/Haiphong. Be prepared to extend operations past three days if directed.' Plans called for the B-52s to attack at night, from 30–35,000ft, with Air Force F-111A and USN A-6A aircraft following up by day. All available B-52s would strike against thirty-four previously restricted targets, against rail yards, power plants, communications facilities, air defence radars, Haiphong's docks, oil storage complexes and ammunition supply areas – over 60 per cent of them within a 25-mile radius of Hanoi, which were to be bombed in any weather using radar rather than visual aiming. SAC retained control over the choice of targets and also drew up

◀ Memorial tablet describing the shooting down of *Cobalt 1* by SAMs fired by Battalion 72, Regiment 285 Air Defence Missile (Hero) Unit at 23.05 on 27 December 1972. The carcass fell on Hoa Tham Street and Ngoc Ha Flower Village area in Ba Dinh district, Hanoi. (Author)

INTRODUCTION ON REMAINS OF HOA LO PRISON

Late of 19th century, the French colonialist intensified the machine of suppression such as: adding police forces, completing the lawcourt system, building the prison net... in order to cope with Vietnamese struggle movements. Hoa Lo prison was built in 1896 in Phu Khanh village, Vinh Xuong canton, Tho Xuong district, Hanoi. This was one of the biggest prison built by the French colonialist in Indochina.

The French colonialist changed Hoa Lo from a famous trade village specialized in producing ceramic into a prison where confined and persecuted both the body and the mind of thousands of revolutionary patriotic soldiers. Many leaders of the Government and Vietnam Communist Party were imprisoned here.

Living in the imperialistic prison, under a severe punishment and maltreated life but revolutionary patriotic soldiers still kept steady their sense of purpose and uprightness, turned the prison into the school where propagated revolutionary argument. Many soldiers ingeniously escaped from the prison to come back with the organisation, with people and made appropriate contribution to the cause of liberation the motherland.

In October 1954, after the North was liberated, Hoa Lo prison was temporary managed and used by Vietnamese Government to keep law breakers. From 5 August 1964 to 29 March 1973, Hoa Lo prison was used to remand in custody American pilots who were shot down or arrested when bombing the North of Vietnam.

In 1993, in order to meet the cultural developmental needs of the Capital, Vietnamese Government decided to change the using aim of this prison. The South-East side of the prison was kept, embellished and classified as revolutionary relic of Hanoi. Here also located a monument to revolutionary patriotic soldiers who heroically lay down in Hoa Lo prison for the independence and freedom of the nation.

the plans for the direction of attack and the bomb loads to be carried.

B-52D/G attacks on Hanoi were to begin at about 1900 hours Hanoi time on 17 December, but Nixon moved LINEBACKER II back twenty-four hours to the night of 18/19 December due to fears of offending the Chinese who hosted a political visit by North Vietnam on the 17th. In any event, not enough KC-135A tankers were in position to refuel the planned sorties by B-52s from Guam. The bombing campaign would begin during some of the worst weather of the year: the middle of the north-east monsoon. Low cloud covered the Hanoi region for most of the day. The

▲ Tablet describing the infamous 'Hanoi Hilton'. (Author)

◄ The notorious 'Hanoi Hilton' where USAF PoWs were imprisoned during the Vietnam War. (Author)

general staff briefing noted an ominous stand-down in B-52 activities in the south and the report radioed by an American weather reconnaissance aircraft flying above the city was intercepted. Hanoi's air defences went on the alert.

At U-Tapao crews crammed briefing rooms to hear Colonel Donald M. Davis tell them, 'Gentlemen, your target for tonight is Hanoi'. At Andersen all of the B-52 crews assembled in the 'D' Complex (ARC LIGHT) briefing room. All came to

Bombs and shells of the US Army on Cuchi Land.

attention when General James McCarthy entered. He would later fly on another LINEBACKER II strike as air commander even though he had developed a raging case of pneumonia. 'Reminiscent of *Twelve O'Clock High* episodes,' recalled Captain Robert P. Jacober Jr, 'the briefing officer stepped to the centre of the stage and

◄▲ The VC were masters of improvisation, turning captured American tyres into footwear and converting UXB bombs dropped by B-52s into hand grenades and booby-trap bombs. (Author)

▲ B-52s taxi out on 26 December 1972. (USAF)

said, "Gentlemen, your mission for today is ..." A pause. Then the viewgraph machine projected an image of a small portion of a map on the screen. The map scale was such that "HA" was on one side of the city and "NOI" was on the other. The mind did not fuse the words until the briefing officer said "Hanoi". Dead silence was followed by everyone talking at once. Dramatic and impressive, yes. Scared, yes. Eager, yes. As a combat wing, this was the highest I had ever

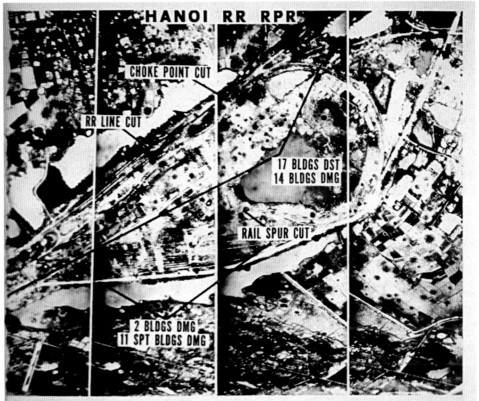

Text labels within image:
HANOI RR RPR
CHOKE POINT CUT
RR LINE CUT
17 BLDGS DST
14 BLDGS DMG
RAIL SPUR CUT
2 BLDGS DMG
11 SPT BLDGS DMG

◄ Bomb Damage Assessment (BDA) photograph of the Hanoi rail yards after the B-52 raids on 26 December 1972. (USAF)

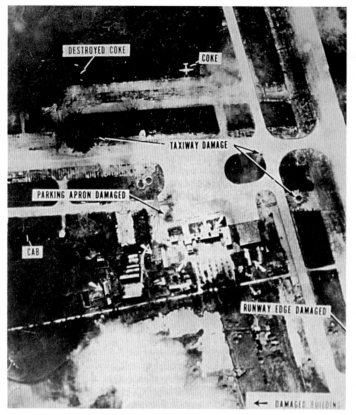

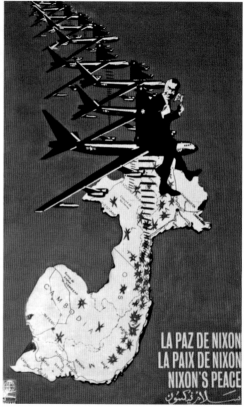

seen morale. We were about to really contribute to the war.'

The first raid would be with 129 B-52s in three waves, with four- to five-hour intervals between each wave. The long time lapses between waves was designed to keep Hanoi's population awake throughout the night, but it would also give SA-2 crews a chance to engage the first attack and then rearm their missile launchers to meet the next two raids. The Guam-based B-52D/G units were to attack forty-eight targets, including the extensive Kinh No storage

◀◀ BDA of Hanoi-Gia Lam airfield after the B-52 raids on 26 December 1972. (USAF)

▶ Dutch anti-war poster displayed in the War Remnants Museum in Saigon. (Author)

◀Anti-war poster, OSPAAAL (Italy) in the War Remnants Museum in Saigon. (Author)

medisch comite nederland · vietnam

helpt waar de bommen vallen

MEDISCHE HULP VOOR NOORD VIETNAM EN DE NATIONALE BEVRIJDINGS-
BEWEGINGEN VAN ZUID VIETNAM, LAOS EN CAMBODJA

POSTGIRO 1090400

► 15,000lb bomb on display at the War Remnants Museum in Saigon. (Author)

►► North Vietnamese map showing B-52 routes used to bomb Hanoi. (Author)

area north of Hanoi which contained four key targets, and the rail yards at Yen Vien, all in the Hanoi area. Because of their shorter endurance the 'Wild Weasels' and other support aircraft could stay in the target area for about an hour only, so the support packages had to be split into three groups rather than operating as one large force. The first wave of forty-eight B-52D/Gs would arrive just after dark, the second wave of thirty aircraft would strike at midnight and the fifty-one aircraft of the third wave would attack Hanoi at 0400 hours on the morning of the 19th. Seven cells made up of twenty-one aircraft from U-Tapao were detailed to bomb MiG-21 *Fishbed* bases at Hòa Lac, Kep and Phuc Yen.

As they were bussed to their waiting bombers, *Wave II*, which would begin taking off at 1900 hours, received their briefing. Lieutenant-Colonel Hendsley R. Conner and his staff had worked

TRẬN ĐÁNH B52 CỦA TÊN LỬA Ở KHU VỰC HÀ NỘI ĐÊM 18 RẠNG 19-12-1972

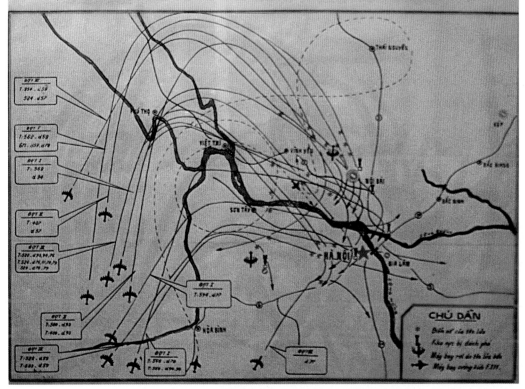

almost around the clock getting the schedule prepared, notifying the crews, ordering meals and the transportation and preparing flying equipment, so that thirty crews and aircraft plus spares were assigned to *Wave II*. Conner, who had flown over 200 missions in Martin B-57 Canberras and who now commanded one of the provisional squadrons on Guam, was Deputy Airborne Commander (ABC) to the second wave. He would occupy the fold-down jump seat behind Major Cliff Ashley and his co-pilot, Captain Gary Vickers, on the flight deck of B-52G Call Sign *Peach 2*, whose crew were from the 2nd Bomb Wing at Barksdale AFB, Louisiana. Sitting on a jump seat for eleven hours trussed up like a turkey with a 40lb PCU-10P parachute pack is highly uncomfortable. Colonel Conner would have to wear his parachute at all times because the jump seat was not fitted with an

◀ B-52D-80-BO
56-0629 at U-Tapao
RTAB in 1968 bombed
up for another ARC LIGHT
mission. 56-0629 is now
on permanent display
at the 8th Air Force
Museum, Barksdale AFB,
Louisiana. (USAF)

◀◀ B-52Ds over
Vietnam. (USAF)

ejection device. In emergency he would have to disconnect oxygen and intercom, unhitch from his seat, go below and wait to bail out through a hole in the floor of the compartment after the navigators had ejected!

Shortly before departure each crew was given three large, black briefcases full of information, such as Mission 'frag' folders, radar offset aim-points and imagery of target areas divided into 'low threat' and 'high threat' depending on the number

of SA-2s and the risk from MiGs. In order to maintain the sortie rate, crews of six ground-spare B-52s pre-flighted up to the 'engine start' point for 'abort' standby had to be prepared to fill in for any of the three other cells. Each, therefore, received nine 'frag' briefcases. B-52G *Charcoal 3*, Don Rissi's aircraft, was in the fourteenth cell of three aircraft in the first wave, but when *Charcoal 2* was taken out of line because of an equipment malfunction, Rissi's aircraft became *Charcoal 2* and one of the ground-spare B-52s filled in.

◀ B-52F-70-BW 57-0162 dropping M117 bombs over Vietnam. (USAF)

▶ B-52D near a bomb dump during the Vietnam War. (USAF)

B-52s dropping bombs over Vietnam. (USAF)

Rissi and 1st Lieutenant Robert J. 'Bobby' Thomas, his substitute co-pilot, climbed up the ladder rungs of the enormous B-52, grasped the 'fire pole' and scrambled through the floor hatch opening into the narrow corridor to the subterranean flight deck. Physically, the B-52 was cold after several hours of high-altitude flying. The seat cushion did not cushion after several hours and the cockpit was cramped and uncomfortable. Underneath the flight deck Major Richard E. 'Dick' Johnson, the navigator, and Captain Robert G. Certain, the radar navigator, who was also the bombardier who armed the missiles, took their seats in the windowless bombardier-navigator team compartment where, illuminated only by their instruments, they were always busy during the whole flight. Sergeant Walter L. Ferguson, the gunner, took his seat in the forward cabin where a TV camera assisted him in sighting and

Did you know

On the night of 11/12 April 1966, Operation Rock Kick II/Rolling Thunder 50 – the first B-52 mission over North Vietnam – took place when thirty B-52Ds from Guam each dropped twenty-four 1,000lb bombs and twenty-four wing-mounted 750lb bombs from 35,000ft on a 3-mile section of the Mu Gai Pass. It was the largest bombing mission since the Second World War. In all, 600 tons of bombs were dropped on the steep mountain slopes of the Pass, the aim being to cause rockslides to block the route. However, although some damage was caused, the North Vietnamese had the road open again within twenty-four hours.

➤ B-52D-65-BO 55-0110 of the 307th Strategic Wing at U-Tapao, Thailand, with Mk 82 500lb bombs on the underwing pylons and 'C-Clips' of mines on the loading vehicle prior to being loaded into the bomb bay. On 22 November 1972 this was the first B-52 combat loss in Vietnam after two SAMs exploded beneath the bomber just after it dropped its bombs on enemy troops at Vinh. The crew ejected safely after crossing the Mekong River into Thailand. (USAF)

➤➤ B-52 *Litening* pod. (Hal Rigg via Buck Rigg)

he operated the tail gun position remotely. (On the B-52D tail turret the gunner was particularly effective in being able to monitor SA-2 SAM missile launches and approaching MiGs from the rear.) Ferguson and Captain Richard T. 'Tom' Simpson, the electronic warfare officer (EWO), or 'E-Dub' (the intercom call sign for EW), faced backwards, so their ejection seats were equipped with a 'hatch lifter', which would convert the hatch above them into an air brake and hold it out of the way while they ejected upwards or climbed out. In an emergency the pilots would eject upwards, and the navigator and radar navigator would eject downwards. If the pilots' seats failed they had to unhitch and shin down the 'fire pole' to the bombardier-navigator team compartment and bail out.

'For this mission,' recalled Captain Jacober, 'crews pre-flighted the bombs and equipment a little bit more thoroughly, followed the checklist a little more closely, imagining what it would be like, and would you panic. Everyone was offered extra .38 ammo; only our gunner took more. He took two extra boxes. We still don't know what he was going to do with all that ammo.'

Every part of Andersen AFB was full to the brim with aircraft and personnel, for the number of men needed to maintain and fly the B-52s was enormous. The B-52s were lined up, nose to tail, along the narrow taxiway, waiting their turn to use the 2-mile-long runway oriented west to east: tyres squeaking, engines belching JP-4 laden fumes, brakes complaining, crews sweating, radios filled with marshalling instructions, a tight nervous feeling among everyone concerned. At 1451 local time Major Bill Stocker, who had already logged 300 B-52 combat sorties, led the procession of bombers down the uneven runway. The B-52s' engines were

◄ 461st Bomb Wing crew at U-Tapao preparing for a mission over Vietnam. (Hal Rigg via Buck Rigg)

boosted with water-injection for take-off and as Stocker took off he left eight wakes of smoke in the sky behind. Every ninety seconds another fully loaded B-52 rolled down the runway. The most dangerous part of the mission was watching the last 1,000ft of runway approach as the pilot tried to get a 480,000lb aircraft into the air. After a number of B-52s had taken off the sky was full of smoke as there was not enough wind to clear it away. Off the coast at Andersen a Russian trawler counted the bombers as they took off and broadcast the information to North Vietnam. Each B-52 cleared the cliff which loomed after take-off and then made a precipitous drop of several hundred feet into the ocean as if falling into the sea. Onlookers watched aircraft struggle to become airborne just before reaching the visible rim of the island, only to drop out of sight momentarily and then climb away. *Charcoal 1* lost four engines on one side soon after take-off. Its pilot, Captain Goodman, managed to land safely. Rissi now assumed the leading aircraft in *Charcoal* cell as *Charcoal 2* became *Charcoal 1*. Another B-52 suffered a refuelling system failure outbound. One crew, which lost an engine, were told to push up the power, stay with the formation and pick up extra fuel on the return leg.

Captain Jacober recalled, 'Crossing the pond westbound was the usual boredom. But spirits were high. There was some kidding. The gunner was bragging how he was going to get a MiG. The return trip was going to be more subdued, introspective.'

* * *

In Hanoi, General Vo Ngoyen Giap learned that B-52s had taken off from Guam and Thailand; the latter had been detected flying northward along the Mekong River. The bombers from Andersen flew over the Pacific and into South Vietnam, then through Laos where they joined Thailand-based B-52s and formed into one long line of aircraft in groups of three. With up to ten minutes between each three-aircraft cell the B-52s stretched over 70 miles of sky. The procession continued north towards the Chinese border before turning east into North Vietnam. Then they headed south-east down the Tam Đào mountain range, known to US pilots as 'Thud Ridge', to Hanoi.

The crews, who were unfamiliar with flying in large formations at night, were under orders to manoeuvre as little as possible to avoid collisions, and the stream of three-aircraft cells was compressed to help preserve the mutual ECM protection and keep the B-52s within the *Chaff* corridors that were laid in the Hanoi area to interfere with enemy radar frequencies.

If the SA-2s' *Spoon Rest* long-range target acquisition radar or the *Fan Song* shorter-range missile guidance system locked on to a B-52, the American crews were to break off their attacks and head for a secondary target. (*Fan Song* got its name from its horizontal and vertical fan scanning antennas and its distinctive sounding emissions, which could be picked up by the B-52s' warning equipment.) But this and other factors limited the approach and exit routes available to the B-52s. The south-east target approach was to take advantage of the 100-knot jet stream tailwind blowing from the north-west, but the winds to a large extent dispersed the chaff. In any case, the North Vietnamese tactic of firing a proportion of the SA-2 missiles without guidance meant that the effectiveness of the chaff was limited.

Only about fifty-seven of the ninety-eight Guam-based B-52Gs had received the

► Pre-loaded M117 bombs waiting to be attached to the underwing pylons of B-52Ds on Guam during the Vietnam War. (Boeing)

updates to their ECM equipment and Rissi's was one that hadn't. Yet all the B-52Ds had. EWOs in single B-52s could operate their countermeasures to defeat single missiles, but they were hard-pressed to identify and individually jam missiles fired at the bomber stream in a shotgun pattern, as they often were. The Vietnamese simply tripped off salvoes of six missiles from each site. The lighter structure of the B-52G, which contributed to its outstanding long-range performance and in turn reduced the need for aerial refuelling, meant that the aircraft was more vulnerable to battle damage. The B-52s were especially vulnerable just prior to bomb release (the radar signature of the B-52 increased significantly when the bomb doors were opened) and after, when they were to swing in wide turns to the west and head back over Laos, which, it was hoped, would take them out of SAM range as soon as possible. Conventional B-52 bombing techniques in Vietnam were identical to the procedures laid down in training for nuclear strikes whereby SAC crews executed a 45° banked turn known as the 'post target

▲ 461st Bomb Wing crew at U-Tapao next to their B-52. (Hal Rigg via Buck Rigg)

◄◄ B-52 crew in Vietnam. (USAF)

◄ B-52D en route to its target in March 1965. (Hal Rigg via Buck Rigg)

turn' (or PTT) to escape a nuclear blast. These steep turns blanked out the jamming antennas on the undersides of the B-52s. Requests by the 8th Air Force to allow B-52 crews to flatten out the turn to 15° of bank had fallen on deaf ears at SAC.

Did you know?
In South-East Asia the B-52, or High Altitude Plough or Aluminum Overcast, was universally known as the 'Buff' (Big Ugly Fat F**ker) – an acronym applied derisively by fighter pilots aware of the aura of invincibility associated with B-52 crews who were under orders to avoid losses even if it meant breaking off a bombing run when threatened by SAM missiles.

The B-52 streams were preceded by F-111As tasked with attacking MiG fighter bases. One of the F-111s was shot down and one MiG was subsequently shot down by a B-52G gunner but the greatest danger was from SAMs. As the bombers closed in on their targets the North Vietnamese defences began to react. Even though the North Vietnamese defences had been degraded they still managed to fire off an estimated 200 missiles. Captain Robert E. Wolf, the pilot of one of the B-52s operating from Guam, recalled, 'From the beginning of the bomb run to the target, my gunner counted 32 SAMs fired at or at least passing close to our aircraft.' Captain Robert P. Jacober added, 'My first real sense of combat was not the flashes ahead – that would prove to be the SAMs detonating – but the sound of multiple "beepers"; the emergency locator radio beacons that are activated by a parachute opening after an ejection. So many going off at once could only signify that a BUFF had been shot down. The only advice I could remember was, if you can keep a SAM moving across your windscreen, it is not going to hit you.'

Lilac 3, piloted by Major David O'Neil, was hit near the left side of the cockpit by a SAM explosion, which punctured most of the fuel tanks, knocked out the instruments and electrical power, and damaged the bomb-release system. O'Neil had been hit by small pieces of shrapnel in his eye and arms, and Joe Grega, the co-pilot, was hit in both arms. In the rear of the aircraft, gunner Joe Smart's compartment had been hit heavily and all his oxygen lines were cut. There was a large hole the size of a small plate in the back of his seat but miraculously Smart was uninjured in the blast. With the loss of fuel in the drop tank the B-52D began rolling rapidly to the right before both pilots got it under control.

Lilac 3 diverted to U-Tapao, leaking fuel and with all radios and the intercom out. Unbeknown to the crew, the bleed air duct in the bomb bay had ruptured and was pouring 800° bled air from the engines on to the full load of 750lb bombs still in the bomb bay. Grega managed to put *Lilac 3* down at U-Tapao where the bombs were too hot to touch with bare hands and ground crew stopped counting after the holes in the aircraft 'reached 680'.

On *Peach 2* the first report Hendsley Conner heard was from Colonel Thomas F. Rew, commander of the 72nd Strategic Wing (P), who made his call-in after they exited the target area. Conner, who had got very little rest the night before due to the many problems that had come up during mission planning, had managed to get three hours' sleep before the co-pilot woke him up for their in-flight refuelling. When the refuelling was over, Conner tuned in the

➤ B-52D-30-BW 56-0658 of the 461st Bomb Wing at U-Tapao in 1965. (Hal Rigg via Buck Rigg)

radio to hear how the lead wave was doing. By now they were in the target area and he should be able to hear how the enemy was reacting. Rew said they had had 'a tough experience'. One aircraft was known to be shot down by SAMs, two were presently not accounted for and one had received heavy battle damage. He initially estimated that the North Vietnamese had fired over 200 SAMs at them. There were no reports of MiG fighter attacks. The anti-aircraft artillery was heavy but well below their flight level.

In Hanoi, General Vo Ngoyen Giap was informed that a B-52 had been shot down by a unit of the 261st Missile Regiment.

The Initial Point-to-Target axis of attack took *Charcoal 1* and Don Rissi's crew over the most closely grouped SAM sites defending Hanoi. B-52 bombing computers required an absolutely straight and level approach and crews had to maintain that

approach for at least four minutes before dropping their bombs. If radar navigators were not entirely sure of their targets at this point they were instructed to abort their

▲ Loading a B-52D of the 461st Bomb Wing with wing-mounted bombs at U-Tapao in 1965. (Hal Rigg via Buck Rigg)

► Already a veteran of thirty combat missions, B-52D-80-BO 56-0617 prepares to add bomb symbol 31 upon its safe return. (Hal Rigg via Buck Rigg)

drop. As *Charcoal 1* ran in on the Yen Vien rail yards it received a near-direct SAM hit the instant the bomb doors were opened. Rissi, Bobby Thomas and Walt Ferguson were killed as the aircraft exploded in a ball of fire. Dick Johnson managed to salvo the 27,750lb bombs in the bomb bay before he ejected. Bob Certain and Tom Simpson ejected also. They were taken prisoner, with Johnson being paraded through the streets of Hanoi for propaganda value on the world's TV news bulletins.

For Hendsley Conner the worst part was: 'now the North Vietnamese knew that they were coming' and when he reached the target 'things probably would be even worse'. Conner thought he knew what was in store for them but he had never seen so many SAMs. 'They made white streaks of light as they climbed into the night sky. As they left the ground, they would move slowly, pick up speed as they climbed, and end their flight, finally, in a cascade of sparkles.' There were so many of them it reminded Conner of 'a Fourth of July fireworks display. A beautiful sight to watch if I hadn't known how lethal they could be.' He did not feel nearly as secure in the big, lumbering bomber as he had in his B-57 Canberra that could manoeuvre much better.

Peach 2 had just released its bombs on the Yen Vien rail yards when, near Kinh No, a SAM exploded just off the left wing. The detonation blew the wing tip and external fuel tank completely off and set the two outboard engines on fire. Cliff Ashley and Gary Vickers nursed *Peach 2* 250 miles to friendly territory with wing and engine fires taking hold. Two F-4s joined them as they crossed the Mekong River into Thailand and one of the Phantom pilots, seeing that the fire was getting worse, 'suggested' that Ashley's crew ejected rather than ride it out to an emergency field. The red 'Abandon' light came on. Conner unhitched from his seat, shinned down the 'fire pole' and bailed out through one of the holes in the floor of the bombardier-navigator team compartment left by 1st Lieutenant Forrest Stegelin and Major Archie Myers, the radar navigator who had ejected. All the crew, including the EWO, Captain Jim Trammel and gunner Master Sergeant Ken Connor, abandoned the aircraft near a USMC base at Nam Phong and within twenty minutes 'Jolly Green' rescue helicopters had picked them all up.

Having lost the element of surprise *Wave III*, which arrived nearly five hours after the second wave to attack the Kinh No Complex, the Hanoi railroad repair shops at Gia Lam and the main radio station on the outskirts of Hanoi, was met with a formidable defensive array of sixty-one SAMs fired, heavy AAA fire and MiG-21s attempting interceptions. Seven B-52D cells flying in from almost due west came within range of eleven SAM sites. *Rainbow 01* was slightly damaged. Captain Hal K. 'Red' Wilson, who with his crew was deployed from the 99th Bomb Wing at Westover AFB, Massachusetts, was *Rose 1*, the lead aircraft in the last cell to bomb the radio station. Wilson, who was flying his 251st combat mission over South-East Asia after four tours of duty, recalled that SAMs were 'wall to wall'. *Rose 1* was almost downed on its post-target turn when a SAM went between the wing and the stabiliser. A second SAM detonated at the B-52D's height of 38,000ft and knocked out the No. 3 and 4 engines. As *Rose 1* hurtled down in the vicinity of Hanoi, Wilson and co-pilot Captain Charles A. Brown Jr both ejected. The radar navigator, Major Fernando Alexander, who had joined the Air Force in 1952 and had been a navigator on B-29s and B-47s prior to converting to the B-52, looked through a large hole on the left side of the aircraft at the external bomb rack and saw the No. 3 engine on fire. He, too, ejected. Captain Henry 'Hank' C. Barrows, a German whose family had immigrated to the USA in 1958, became the fourth member of the crew to be taken prisoner. He had previously flown 120 missions during a tour on the AC-130 Hercules gunship at Ubon.

Captain Robert P. Jacober continued:

We had already been warned that MiGs had launched and were heading our way. The EWO alerted us that SAM radars were following us. There was a cloud layer beneath us, so when I saw the first SAM ignite on the launcher, the plume was diffused like a match seen through a fog. But it quickly focused into a sharp flame, and the SAM looked like someone was throwing a candle at us. Seven were launched at us during the bomb run, four on our inbound run and three over the city. We could determine that only one was guided. It came at us from our twelve o'clock position. The EWO said 'Uplink' about the time I saw it come up through the clouds. No matter what the pilot did, we could not get it to move on the windscreen. It passed just off of our nose and exploded several thousand feet above us. If they had had our altitude right, we probably would have been hit. The bomb run itself went as briefed. Our post-target turn took us among the four SAM sites that were in downtown Hanoi. During the turn, the pilot had rolled into about 70° of bank. We lost several thousand feet. Since I was looking almost straight down, I had a good view of the three SAMs that launched. Fortunately none came close, and the return flight to Guam was quiet.

The three losses were considered acceptable losses but morale slumped to a low ebb indeed on the third night, 20/21 December, when ninety-nine B-52D/Gs in thirty-three cells took off from Thailand and Guam and headed for Hanoi again. In nine hours, 220 SAMs were fired at the B-52s and six of those despatched – four of them unmodified B-52Gs – were lost to SA-2 strikes, with seventeen men killed or MIA and nine taken prisoner.

Captain Rolland A. Scott flew *Gold 2*. As he passed east of NKP (Nakhon Phanom, Thailand) on a southerly heading the crew heard a B-52 crew abandoning their aircraft over friendly territory. 'In the distance toward NKP,' recalled Scott, 'we soon saw a fireball which we assumed to be a "Buff" impacting the ground. It must have been *Brass 2* and Captain John Ellinger and his crew were mighty lucky.' *Brass 2* had three jammers out of action so to keep the radar signature to a minimum, Ellinger did not open his bomb bay doors until just fifteen seconds before the target, but he could do nothing when two SAMs were fired as they were on their right post-target turn. The first SAM exploded off *Brass 2*'s right wing and the second detonated just off the right side. The explosions knocked out the B-52G's electrical power, damaged the controls and put the four engines on the right side out of action. Ellinger and his co-pilot nursed the crippled bomber to Thailand where all six crew ejected safely at around 10,000ft near Nakhon Phanom.

The crew of *Orange 3*, captained by Major John Franklin Stuart, heard the emergency beepers from the crew of *Quilt 3* as they started their bomb run on Yen Vien. Just seconds before bomb release, the B-52D was attacked by a MiG-21, resulting in damage and a small fire in the forward

◄ B-52D-60-BO
55-0100 completed
5,000 ARC LIGHT hours
in Vietnam and became
a fitting memorial to the
men lost on operations
when it was put on
display at Andersen AFB,
Guam, before being
scrapped in 1983 due to
corrosion. (USAF)

wheel well. Between fifteen and twenty SAMs were fired at *Orange* cell while in the target area and a volley of three SAMs was fired at *Orange 3* at 35,500ft about 5 miles north of Hanoi; *Orange 3* received at least one direct hit in the bomb bay just before bombing while the rest of the cell was on its post-target turn. The aircraft went into a flat spin with its starboard wing on fire and pieces falling off the aircraft.

The cabin depressurised and the electrical power failed so the aircraft commander ordered the crew to abandon the aircraft, which then crashed in Yen Thuong village. The B-52D exploded in a ball of fire, which could be seen 80 miles away over the Gulf of Tonkin by the crew of a RC-135. Captain Klomann and 1st Lieutenant Granger survived the explosion and they managed to eject. Klomann was seriously injured and remained semi-conscious for two weeks but was nursed back to health by his fellow PoWs. SAM units had shot down three of the B-52s in less than ten minutes using just thirty-five missiles.

A SAM detonated close to B-52D *Brick 02* commanded by Captain John Mize as he completed his post-target turn. Mize landed at U-Tapao with nineteen holes in the aircraft and a large piece of shrapnel in the EW station at head level. If the EW had not been leaning forward over his jammers at the time he would have been decapitated.

In three days over 300 sorties had been flown and nine aircraft lost. Statistically, the overall loss rate of 3 per cent was acceptable but the losses on 20/21 December were 9 per cent for the night. General Meyer and his senior officers were stunned at the news. A high loss rate and the increased operational turnaround would lead to crew fatigue and maintenance problems and missions could not then be sustained indefinitely. Crews were on duty sixteen hours at a stretch. After this costly night the unmodified B-52Gs were not sent on raids over Hanoi again.

Two more B-52s were shot down the following night and Hanoi was removed from the target list. For three nights in a row up until Christmas Eve there were no further losses. Nixon ordered a thirty-six-hour bombing halt for Christmas but when

B-52 operations resumed again on the night of 26/27 December, two more B-52s were shot down taking total losses to thirteen.

On 27/28 December sixty B-52D and Gs supported by 101 USAF and USN aircraft were sent to bomb targets close to Hanoi. Seven cells were allocated Lang Đàng rail yard and three cells targeted Duc Noi, while four cells were given Trung Quang rail centre near Hanoi and two cells the van Diem supply complex. One cell each was given three SAM sites. Altogether, 120 SAMs were launched and they hit two B-52s. *Ash 2* crashed in Thailand and all the crew ejected safely.

For Captain John Mize, commander of B-52D 56-0599 *Ash-2*, who was to bomb the SAM site at VN 243, it was third time unlucky. Mize stood *Ash 2* almost on its wing during the post-target turn as a salvo of SAMs were fired at the formation. One hit the B-52 in the left wing and knocked out all four engines on that side and two were on fire. Mize managed to keep the aircraft aloft for almost an hour before the bomb bay doors fell open and one of the landing gear began to cycle, lowering then retracting. Mize knew that he was losing his hydraulic system and the B-52's descent steepened with the sudden increase in drag. Mize saw the lights of Nakhon Phanom and told the crew to eject. Everyone eventually

Did you know?

The LINEBACKER II eleven-day campaign in December 1972 was the heaviest of the war in South-East Asia and fifteen B-52s came down, or crashed, as a result of being hit by SAMs. Three B-52s were seriously damaged and six had minor damage. No fewer than 1,242 SAMs had been fired at the B-52s.

exited the aircraft safely, though navigator Bill Robinson's ejection seat failed and he was forced to unstrap and bail out through the hole left by the radar navigator's seat. Mize was awarded the Air Force Cross.

A total of about forty-five SAMs were fired at the B-52s that approached Hanoi. One minute before bomb release on the railway yards at Trung Quang, *Cobalt 1* was locked on to by two SAMs at 25,000ft. Captain Frank Lewis and his co-pilot, Captain Samuel B. Cusimano, evaded these but they were not able to dodge a third missile that struck the B-52 as it was in a tight turn near Bac Ninh, 15 miles north-east of Hanoi. All the crew were injured to some extent by the explosion and 1st Lieutenant Bennie L. Fryer was almost certainly killed at this point. The wings caught fire, the fuel tanks were ruptured and the electrical system failed. Forty seconds after being hit and unable to release his bombs, Lewis gave the order to abandon the aircraft. He, Cusimano and Major James Carroll Condon ejected safely before the aircraft crashed. Master Sergeant James W. Gough was hit by pieces of burning debris from the engines and wings as he left the gun turret before the aircraft disintegrated. Major Allen Louis Johnson, the EWO, was thought to have ejected from the aircraft. A North Vietnamese interrogator told Lewis that he knew his navigator was a black man, indicating either that he had been captured or that his body had been found. Cusimano had flown 144 missions in C-123K flare ships from Nakhon Phanom before assignment to B-52s. Condon had amassed over 6,000 hours in SAC B-47s and B-52s, and had flown over 120 missions during the war.

Operations north of the 20th Parallel ceased at midnight on 29 December. *Cobalt 1* was the fifteenth and final loss of the

LINEBACKER II campaign. In eleven days, B-52s flew 729 sorties against 34 targets. About 884 SAMs were fired at the B-52s and 24 achieved hits. Of the 24, 15 resulted in downed aircraft. There were 92 crew members aboard these 15 aircraft. Sixty-one of these (28 killed; 33 taken prisoner) went down over North Vietnam. Of the 31 crew who made it to Laos or Thailand, 25 lived. Over 130,000 tons of bombs had hit targets, mainly with precision, but 1,318 civilians died in Hanoi and 305 were killed in Haiphong. The four survivors of *Cobalt 1* were released on 29 March 1973. Lieutenant Fryer's remains were returned by the North Vietnamese on 30 September 1977 and Major Johnson's were returned on 4 December 1985 and formally identified the following June. Wreckage from the aircraft can still be seen on the surface of a pond at Ngoc Ha, Ba Dinh district, Hanoi. The North Vietnamese have kept it that way.

Did you know?
During the war in South-East Asia, June 1965 – 15 August 1973, 126,615 B-52 sorties were flown, 9,800 of them against North Vietnam. Of these, 124,499 reached their targets, with 124,532 B-52s successfully dropping their bombs. In all, 2,633,035 tons of bombs were dropped. Fifty-five per cent of the sorties flown were against targets in South Vietnam, 27 per cent against targets in Laos, 12 per cent in Cambodia and 6 per cent in North Vietnam. In total, twenty-six B-52s, including four B-52s in collisions, were lost.

During the Cold War, when the threat of nuclear war was at its most prominent, the B-52 came to symbolise America's nuclear defence posture against the Soviet Union. Strategic Air Command (SAC) was created on 21 March 1946 to conduct long-range offensive operations in any part of the world. In-flight refuelling was introduced, giving SAC bombers true intercontinental range. Development of the B-52 had begun in June 1945 after the AAF had directed Air Material Command to consider second-generation intercontinental bombers to eventually replace the B-36 Peacemaker in post-war service. On 23 November 1945 a series of specifications was issued calling for a bomber with an operating radius of 5,000 miles and a speed of 300mph at 34,000ft. The crew was to be five, plus gunners for an undetermined number of 20mm cannon turrets. A 10,000lb bomb load was specified, as well as provisions for a six-man relief crew. On 13 February 1946 the new bomber requirement was circulated among the aviation giants. Boeing's proposal was the turboprop-powered Model 462 which looked like a larger version of the wartime B-29 Superfortress. The Model 462 failed to meet the range requirement, but in mid-June 1946 a new design, the XB-52, which was to be powered by eight Westinghouse XJ40-13-12 turbojets in underwing podded pairs, appeared. It had a maximum speed of 507mph at 47,000ft. The project survived in no small measure to the efforts of Lieutenant-General Curtis E. LeMay, who transferred from the US Air Forces in Europe (USAFE) to assume command of Strategic Air Command on 19 October 1948. He came out strongly in favour of the B-52 project. Early on

During the Cold War, SAC's fleet of B-52s were at a moment's readiness to make a one-way trip to targets in the Soviet Union; SAC's motto was 'Peace is our Profession'. (Author)

in the B-52 development he insisted the Stratofortress must be able to carry a large conventional as well as nuclear payload, and he was instrumental in getting side-by-side seating arrangement for the pilots instead of the tandem approach adopted on the Boeing B-47B Stratojet. During his nine-year tenure (1948–57), SAC became the world's most powerful military force operating on a global basis. In March 1949

▲ YB-52-BO 49-231 became the first B-52 to fly, on 15 April 1952. (Boeing)

LeMay proposed that SAC's capabilities be increased to the point where it would be possible to deliver 133 atomic bombs against seventy major Soviet cities in a single, all-out strike. This plan was accepted in December 1949 by the Air Force. When

on 30 June 1957 LeMay left to become Air Force Vice Chief of Staff, his legacy to SAC was a strategic air force that had become the only American nuclear deterrent to prevent a pre-emptive Communist strike on the USA. And it was the B-52 that formed

➤ B-52C-45-BO 54-2668, the sixty-eighth Seattle-built B-52. All thirty-five B-52C models delivered were operated by the 42nd Bomb Wing at Loring AFB, Maine, and two squadrons of the 99th Bomb Wing at Westover AFB, Massachusetts. The 42nd Bomb Wing's B-52Cs were disposed of in 1957 and replaced with B-52Ds. (Boeing)

the backbone of the manned bomber strategic deterrent. LeMay was determined to modernise his strategic bombing force with the B-52 and on 9 January 1951, USAF Chief of Staff General Hoyt S. Vandenberg approved a proposal that the B-52 be acquired as a replacement for the B-36.

On 14 February 1951 a contract for an initial batch of thirteen B-52As to be delivered at the beginning of April 1953 was

◀ The three 93rd Bomb Wing B-52B-35-BOs of Operation POWER FLITE at March AFB, California, after they successfully completed a 24,325-mile, globe-circling flight in forty-five hours and nineteen minutes, 16–18 January 1957. (Boeing)

➤ B-52C-40-BO 53-0400. The first B-52C flew on 9 March 1956. In 1971 most B-52Cs were scrapped. Some remained a few years longer, the last aircraft ending its flying career with the Air Force Flight Test Center at Edwards AFB, California, in July 1975. (Boeing)

signed. (Only three B-52As were actually built; the rest were completed as B-52Bs.) By late 1951 the two B-52 prototypes were ready for roll-out. Both had been ordered originally as XB-52s but the second aircraft was re-designated as YB-52 after the 1949 proposal had recommended installing some operational equipment so it could serve as a production prototype.

The YB-52 prototype (49-231) became the first B-52 to fly, on 15 April 1952, from Boeing Field in Seattle to Moses Lake AFB, Washington. Boeing's chief test pilot A.M. 'Tex' Johnston and Lieutenant-

Colonel Guy M. Townsend of the USAF Air Research and Development Command were at the controls. Testing revealed some problems initially with engine reliability. The Pratt & Whitney J57s were prone to surge when normal throttle movements were undertaken at high altitude with low-engine inlet temperatures and there was a tendency to pitch up and roll to starboard when approaching the stall. The braking system was unable to bring the Stratofortress to a halt within the required distance. More than three years of flight-testing went into the XB-52, YB-52, three B-52As and ten B-52Bs before the aircraft were ready for delivery to the USAF, which in summer 1953 agreed plans for a total procurement of 282 B-52s, enough to equip seven bomb wings in SAC, each with an establishment of about thirty aircraft. A total of nine and a half years elapsed from when the basic requirement was established by the Air

Force to when the first operational aircraft was delivered. The balance of the 744 total B-52s produced would be delivered during the following 7.33 years.

No B-52As entered service with the Air Force. Deliveries of the first operational version, the B-52B, which went to the 93rd

▲ Line-up of B-52Ds at Seattle in the mid-1950s. (Boeing)

General Curtis E. LeMay, head of SAC, saw to it that the B-52 had to be able to carry a large conventional as well as nuclear payload and changed Boeing's proposed tandem pilot seating to a side-by-side seating arrangement.

Bombardment Wing, did not begin until 29 June 1955 when the first (52-8711) was accepted. On 8 January 1955 the 4017th Combat Crew Training Squadron was activated and performed all B-52 crew training for the 93rd and for two additional B-52 wings – the 42nd at Loring AFB, Maine, with B-36s, and the 99th at Westover AFB, Massachusetts, with B-47s. In September 1955 SAC planned for 576 B-52s, equipping eleven wings each with forty-five aircraft in three squadrons. The 93rd Bomb Wing was only declared combat ready on 12 March 1956. The last of the B-52Bs was delivered in August; B-52Ds began reaching SAC in June 1956 and the final five B-52Cs reached the Air Force in December.

By December 1956 SAC had upped the procurement requirement to a total of 603 B-52s. In 1957 the first B-52Ds went to the 42nd Bomb Wing at Loring AFB, Maine, where they replaced B-52Cs. All 170 production models were delivered by November 1957 and they equipped five wings in SAC, which had three more wings awaiting delivery of 100 B-52Es. B-52Es first entered service with SAC in December 1957 but production problems with the B-52F delayed its entry until June 1958. By the close of 1957, five B-52 wings with three squadrons each had been activated and another three wings were in the process of re-equipping. In 1958 the number of B-52 wings SAC required was increased to fourteen with forty-two squadrons. By 1 June 1958 SAC included four numbered air forces (2nd, 8th, 15th and 16th) and three direct-reporting air divisions under the command of General Thomas S. Power, who had taken over from General LeMay on 1 July 1957.

One of the most significant B-52 flights was Operation POWER FLITE, 16–18 January 1957, when three B-52Bs (with two reserve aircraft) of the 93rd Bomb Wing carried out a non-stop, round-the-world flight. The 24,325-mile, globe-circling flight was accomplished in forty-five hours and nineteen minutes. General LeMay was there to personally present the crews with the Distinguished Flying Cross. He said that the flight was a 'demonstration of SAC's capabilities to strike at any target on the face of the earth'. POWER FLITE was recognised as the outstanding mission of the year and the 93rd Bomb Wing was awarded SAC's sixth Mackay Trophy.

On 12 April 1960 a B-52G crew in the 4135th Strategic Wing at Eglin AFB, Florida, successfully launched a GAM-77 (AGM-28) Hound Dog air-launched attack missile as the climax of its 20½-hour captive flight to the North Pole and back. The 4135th Strategic Wing had been the first Hound Dog-equipped B-52G unit and first deployed in December 1959. On 14 December that same year a B-52G of the 5th Bomb Wing at Travis AFB, California, completed an official record-breaking flight of 10,078.84 miles without refuelling in nineteen hours and forty-four minutes.

Overcrowding on SAC bases presented tempting targets for Soviet bombers and ICBMs, so a dispersal plan, to reduce vulnerability and ensure survivability of

▲ B-52E-85-BO 56-0635 being refuelled by Boeing KC-135A tanker 57-1467. (Boeing)

Rico. The alert force concept evolved from studies conducted during General LeMay's tenure to investigate ways of avoiding the consequences of a surprise all-out strike by the Soviet Union. SAC planners concluded that one-third of the command's aircraft could be kept on continuous twenty-four-hour alert.

SAC came closest to launching a retaliatory nuclear attack during the Cuban Missile Crisis in mid-October 1962, following Russia's decision to base medium bombers and medium-range and intermediate-range ballistic missiles (IRBMs) on Cuba, just 100 miles from the USA. On Monday evening, 22 October, as President J.F. Kennedy went on national television to announce the presence of missiles on Cuba, SAC cancelled all leaves and put battle staffs on twenty-four-hour operations. Fifty-four B-52s carrying hydrogen bombs took off to join twelve already on airborne alert. One

the nuclear bomber force in the event of a Soviet ICBM missile attack, and a round-the-clock ground (and airborne) alert programme were put in motion. The dispersal programme culminated in 1963 with forty-one B-52 squadrons being distributed among thirty-seven air bases in the Continental USA and one in Puerto

the desired effect. On 24 October shipping carrying the missiles to Cuba came to a stop in the mid-Atlantic and on 28 October the Soviet Union agreed to remove the aircraft from Cuba. By the end of 1960, 428 B-47s, B-52s and B-58s were on alert duty.

◄ B-52G-75-BW 57-6471 *Wolfess* 2 of the 2nd Bomb Wing. (Boeing)

▼ B-52 over a desert air base. (USAF)

of them circled Thule AFB in Greenland to report on any Soviet strike on the early-warning system. US forces in the crisis went to Defense Condition 3. All SAC's 1,519 attack aircraft were loaded with nuclear weapons and as the crisis deepened, SAC's 136 ICBMs were brought to a higher state of alert and fifty-seven B-52s and sixty-one tankers went to DEFCON 2 or continuous airborne alert. No B-52 could land before its replacement aircraft was airborne. The next stage – DEFCON 1 – would mean nuclear war. President Kennedy's 'big stick' had

NB-52E-85-BO 56-0636 which was used as a flying test bed for the XTF99 turbofan, which replaced the starboard inner pair of J57 turbojets. (Boeing)

➤ Ground Alert! (USAF)

Did you know?

On 12 January 1954 John Foster Dulles, the Secretary of State, declared, 'Local defenses must be reinforced by the further deterrent of massive retaliatory power', and that the defence of the West depended 'primarily upon a capacity to retaliate instantly by means and at places of our own choosing'.

In the period 1959–62, follow-on contracts with Boeing increased the total number of B-52s on order to 744. The B-52G flew on 31 August 1958 and entered service with SAC on 13 February 1959. It took the total B-52G procurement to 193 examples, making it the most numerous subtype of the Stratofortress series. The first B-52H flew on 20 July 1960. The B-52H met a requirement to carry four GAM-87A Skybolt missiles on twin missile-launcher pylons. Though the pylons were developed, the B-52s never carried Skybolts operationally, as the missile was cancelled in 1962. The B-52 force reverted to AGM-28 Hound Dogs for a further fourteen years

and the new B-52H models were retrofitted for Hound Dogs in 1963. Deliveries of the B-52H to operational units began on 9 May 1961 when the 379th Bombardment Wing at Wurtsmith AFB, Michigan, received its first aircraft. The last B-52H was delivered in October 1962, bringing production of the Stratofortress to an end. Peak strength was attained in 1963 when 650 B-52s equipped forty-two squadrons at thirty-eight SAC bases. By 1966, when SAC bombers and tankers were heavily involved

B-52E-85-BO 56-0631, the second B-52E, taking off from Seattle. (Boeing)

250 B-1s to replace its ageing B-52s, but the higher-priority long-range Air Launched Cruise Missile (ALCM) programme meant that no new strategic bombers would be built. The B-1A was cancelled in spring 1977 and the B-52G/H became the cruise missile delivery vehicle. By the early 1970s the B-52 had ceased to be a high-level strategic bomber. Almost eighteen years were to elapse after the end of the Vietnam War before the B-52s carried out conventional bombing missions again.

in the war in Vietnam, almost 45 per cent of SAC's 674 bombers (591 of which were B-52s) were on alert.

A B-52 accident in 1968 and an earlier one in Spain hastened the demise of the airborne alert programme whose costs were by now becoming prohibitive. In any event, a large part of the more sophisticated and survivable ICBM force was proving a more cost-effective deterrent. SAC planned for

Did you know?

In November 1956 eight B-52B/Cs of the 93rd and 42nd Bombardment Wings made a non-stop flight around the perimeter of North America in Operation QUICK KICK, covering 12,271 miles in thirty-one hours, thirty minutes.

In the period 1979–81 the yearly totals of just over 400 bombers in SAC included more than 340 B-52s. During 1980–81 SAC demonstrated that it could 'rapidly project US military power to any point in the world in a matter of hours' when B-52s participated in two long-range operations around the globe. In August 1981 the first B-52G modified to carry the Air Launched Cruise Missile, a guided missile that could be launched from wing pylons on the B-52G and deliver a nuclear weapon to a

Saddam Hussein's armies invaded Kuwait. The B-52H units remained on alert in the United States and did not deploy during DESERT STORM. However, once the coalition had gained air superiority, seventy-three B-52Gs participated in DESERT STORM in a conventional role. At first the B-52G force was used for night strikes, employing the Electro-optical viewing system using FLIR (Forward Looking InfraRed) and low-level-light TV sensors to improve low-level night penetration. Then, as air supremacy was gained and areas were found where the air forces could operate without air-to-air threats, the Buffs began operating around the clock. Bombing of airfields and Command, Control & Communications targets would also feature in the B-52Gs' target list.

target 1,500 miles away, was delivered to the 416th Bomb Wing. By the end of 1983 about 260 B-52G/Hs remained active in fifteen wings in SAC.

Conflict in the Persian Gulf began on 1 August 1990, when Iraq's president

At Barksdale AFB on 17 January, seven B-52Gs of the 596th Bomb Squadron, 2nd Bomb Wing, carrying thirty-nine conventionally armed AGM-86B cruise missiles (CALCMs), were used in Project *Senior Surprise* – the bombing of Iraqi targets from the mainland of America. Thirty-five of the CALCMs were launched successfully against the eight high-priority targets in central and southern Iraq, which included a power station at Mosul, the Basrah telephone exchange, and other electrical generating facilities. Four CALCMs failed airborne pre-launch testing, but thirty-one missiles fired hit their targets with precision and the other four exploded close enough to cause serious damage. When the last missile was away, the B-52Gs turned west, re-formed and headed home to air-to-air refuel again with the ever faithful KC-10A Extenders. Two B-52Gs were flying with a pair of seized engines and two other B-52Gs had fluctuating oil pressure readings. In addition, four of the aircraft were carrying 2,500lb hung missiles. It was almost dark when the B-52Gs arrived back at Barksdale but all made it back safely. By the time *Senior Surprise* was over, the B-52G crews had been in the air for over thirty-five hours. It was the longest-ranging combat mission in the history of aerial warfare. (The previous longest-range bombing mission in history was during the

▼ Exposed MD-9 tail gun turret installation on a B-52D. (Frank B. Mormillo)

► Installing six Boeing AGM-86B Air Launched Cruise Missiles on MAU-12 ejector rails of the port 4,450lb ALCM pylon using an ADU-318/E loader adapter. In all, ninety-eight B-52Gs and ninety-five B-52Hs were modified to carry the weapon. (USAF)

Did you know?
In Operation POWER FLITE, on 16–18 January 1957, three B-52Bs of the 93rd Bomb Wing carried out a non-stop, round-the-world flight.

Falklands War. On the night of 30 April/ 1 May 1982 a RAF Vulcan, supported by eleven Victor tankers, made the first *Black Buck* sortie from Ascension Island to Port Stanley airfield in a mission time of fifteen hours and forty-five minutes.)

As in Vietnam a generation earlier, B-52 raids proved a great psychological weapon, especially a few days before the land battle began. Aircraft dropped psychological warfare leaflets to warn Iraqi forces that the B-52s were coming. After the attack, more leaflets reminded the Iraqis where the bombs had come from and said that the B-52s would be back. Most missions against Iraqi targets involved the delivery of up to

Did you know?
In February 1959 it was publically announced that Strategic Air Command had developed a system known as 'airborne alert' where B-52s were in the air twenty-four hours a day, loaded with bombs, on station, ready to go to target.

◀ B-52G-100-BW 58-0204 which was used for the *Rivet Ace* (Phase VI) ECM tests in the early 1970s. (Boeing)

◄ B-52G-90-BW 57-6518 with AGM-69 Short Range Attack Missiles (SRAM). In June 1990 all AGM-69As were removed due to doubts about their safety. (SAC)

► B-52 crew ready for action. (USAF)

◄ B-52G over central Washington State in August 1977. The B-52G was the most numerous subtype with 193 being built exclusively at Boeing Wichita from October 1958 to February 1961. (Boeing)

40,000lb of conventional 'iron' bombs (a co-ordinated weapons release of 153,750lb bombs by a cell of three B-52Gs could wipe out an area 1.5 miles long by 1 mile wide). Despite some inaccuracy, it was estimated that the devastating effects caused by B-52 bombing influenced 20–40 per cent of Iraqis who deserted. Despite their age, the B-52s held a mission-capable rate of more than 80 per cent throughout the war. In all, 102 B-52Gs flew 1,625 sorties (just over 3 per cent of the USA's combat mission total)

▲ B-52H-140-BW
60-0017 in flight. (USAF)

▲▶ B-52H-145-BW
crew member. (USAF)

from their bases in England, Saudi Arabia, Spain and Diego Garcia. They dropped 72,289 bombs for a total of 25,700 tons or 31 per cent of all US bombs (and 41 per cent of the Air Force bombs) dropped during the Gulf War. These are impressive statistics but the results of the B-52 attacks were sometimes disappointing. In post-war analyses, accuracy has been criticised,

Did you know?

On missions in SE Asia, the 4-hour trip over and 4-hour trip back were usually flown by a pilot, safety observer and navigator. The other three crew were often asleep, playing cards or writing etc. For the hour or two that crews were over South Vietnam, they were strapped in tighter.

Did you know?
From 2 March to
30 June 1959
Operation HEAD START
II involved keeping
five B-52Ds of the
92nd Bomb Wing
at Fairchild AFB,
Washington, airborne
at all times. Each
crew flew a twenty-
four-hour sortie. Ten
KC-135s supported
the airborne bombers.

permanent alert posture ended. From September the 'Bomb Wing' or 'Strategic Wing' designations were discarded and the units simply became wings. By the end of 1991 the number of active B-52Gs was down to ninety and these were withdrawn

▲ B-52G-85-BW with T-38A Talon chase plane. (USAF)

due to the high winds, which affected unguided bomb ballistics and caused an error to be introduced by a contractor who misidentified the ground co-ordinates of (some) targets. By 25 February 1991 airpower had forced thousands of Iraqi soldiers to abandon their stockpiles of equipment, weapons and ammunition and surrender.

With the end of the Cold War in sight in late 1991, SAC's B-52 constant,

Did you know?

On 10/11 January 1962 in Operation PERSIAN RUG a B-52H of the 4136th Strategic Wing at Minot AFB set a new distance in a straight line world record by completing an un-refuelled 12,532.28-mile flight from Kadena AB, Okinawa, to Torrejón, Spain. This broke the previous record of 11,235 miles, set in 1946 by the US Navy Lockheed P2V Neptune 'Truculent Turtle'. It flew at altitudes of 40,000 to 50,000ft with a top speed of 662mph.

B-52G-75-BW 57-6471 is refuelled by Boeing KC-135A 58-0004 using a flying boom. (Boeing)

during 1992–93. On 1 June 1992 the B-52G/H fleet was reassigned to the new Air Combat Command (ACC) which was created by amalgamating SAC and Tactical Air Command. By the end of 1992 B-52Gs no longer flew nuclear missions and by early May 1994 all had been retired or were to be broken up for scrap.

In December 1993 the 917th Wing deployed its aircraft, personnel and equipment to Aviana Air Base, Italy, to support the United Nations' no-fly rule over Bosnia-Herzegovina. After Operation DENY FLIGHT, it was decided that three of the five remaining first-line B-52H units would be deactivated by the end of 1994 and their aircraft reassigned to the 2nd and 5th Bomb Wings. The 917th Wing, meanwhile, returned to Aviana Air Base in August 1994 and again in May 1995 to uphold the UN ban on military flights in the Bosnia-Herzegovina airspace. By March

➤ B-52D is refuelled by a Boeing KC-135A using a flying boom. (Boeing)

➤➤ An ALCM launch from a B-52. The B-52H can carry twelve AGM-86B ALCMs externally and eight more internally. (Barksdale AFB)

Did you know?

Airborne alert operations involving B-52s carrying live nuclear bombs ceased in 1968 after a B-52G with four hydrogen bombs on board plunged into the sea ice of North Star Bay at 560mph on 21 January. All four MK28 nuclear weapons detonated, blasting plutonium and uranium over a wide area. A fire fed by 35,000 gallons of jet fuel subsequently destroyed most bomb fragments. A complete MK28 secondary assembly melted through the ice and settled on the sea floor. It has never been retrieved. About 237,000 cubic feet of contaminated ice, snow and water and crash debris was removed during a near eight-month clean-up operation.

1995 the remaining ninety-four H-models were concentrated at just two bases: at Barksdale AFB and Minot AFB in North Dakota. Budgetary cuts in 1996 led to a further reduction in the B-52H fleet with another sixteen B-52Hs being retired. In

Did you know?

Dr Strangelove: or, How I Learned to Stop Worrying and Love the Bomb appeared in 1963. This black comedy about global self-destruction features B-52s and Sterling Hayden, George C. Scott and Peter Sellers (in three roles). Who can ever forget Slim Pickens astride a nuclear bomb rodeo-style as it descends from the bomb bay of a B-52!

➤ B-52D-65-BO 55-0107 tail gun installation. A radome for the MD-9 track antenna was located at the centre of the turret. The glass hemisphere at the top housed the back-up periscopic gun sight, while the larger bulge underneath was for the search antenna. The large white trapezoidal fairing under the gunner's window housed the tail warning radar. (Author)

September 1996 B-52Hs forward based at Andersen AFB, Guam, took part in Operation DESERT STRIKE in Iraq; the bombers returned safely to Guam after a 33.9-hour, 13,600-mile round trip. On 15 September two of the B-52Hs and over 140 personnel re-deployed from Guam to Diego Garcia in case further strike missions were ordered.

◀ B-52H-175-BW 61-0028 *Someplace Special* (right) of the 644th Bomb Squadron, 410th Bomb Wing (H), based at K.I. Sawyer AFB, Michigan, on 16 June 1981 during the RAF Double Top 81/ Giant Strike II RAF/USAF Bombing Competition at RAF Marham, Norfolk, England. (Author)

◀ B-52H-155-BW 60-0046 *Magicians Best* in SAC of the 5th Bomb Wing at RAF Marham, Norfolk, on 16 June 1981. (Author)

▲ B-52H-155-BW 60-0057 of the 644th Bomb Squadron, 410th Bomb Wing, showing a winged fist motif. (Author)

➤ B-52D-20-BW of the 337th Bomb Squadron, 96th Bomb Wing, landing at RAF Marham, 23 September 1981, during Busy Brewer, 1–25 September. (Author)

On 12 October 1996 all 2nd Bomb Wing deployed assets returned to Barksdale. In May 1997 the US Department of Defense decided on a total fleet of 187 bombers, which included just seventy-one B-52Hs, rising to seventy-six when two B-1Bs were lost in accidents; five additional B-52H attrition reserve aircraft were added to the

▲ B-52G-95-BW 58-0185 *El Lobo II* at the USAF Armament Museum, Eglin AFB, Florida. (Author)

Did you know?

In March 1980 two B-52Hs made a non-stop, round-the-world flight in 42½ hours. The flight covered 19,353 nautical miles across Canada, the North Atlantic, Europe, the Mediterranean, the Indian Ocean, the Strait of Malacca, the South China Sea and the North Pacific. Each aircraft received almost 600,000lb of fuel from KC-135 tankers while in flight.

fleet. It was envisaged that 130 bombers, including forty-four B-52Hs, would be available for combat operations at any time.

From 16–19 December 1998 the US and Great Britain launched Operation DESERT FOX – a series of strong, sustained air and cruise missile attacks against military

▲ B-52G-90-BW 57-6508 *Out House Mouse II* of the 2nd Bomb Wing now displayed at Davis-Monthan AFB. (Tony Thornborough)

and suspected NBC related sites in Iraq. During the second and third nights of the attack B-52Hs launched ninety AGM-86C CALCMs against targets in Iraq. On 17 February 1999 the first B-52Hs at Barksdale forward-deployed to RAF Fairford to take part in Operation ALLIED FORCE, a NATO-led operation aimed at bombing Serbia in an attempt to halt the ethnic cleansing of Kosovo and force the Yugoslav army to withdraw from Kosovo. On 24 March six of the B-52Hs took part in the first wave of air strikes, firing CALCMs against Serbian targets. In all, twenty-five individual

◀ B-52G-90-BW
57-6509 *Nine-O-Nine*
at the 8th Air Force
Museum, Barksdale AFB,
Louisiana. (Author)

aircraft deployed during the seventy-eight-day campaign, which lasted from 24 March to 20 June 1999. During fifty-seven days of actual air strikes, the B-52Hs and B-1Bs at RAF Fairford dropped 11,000 bombs and launched sixty-two ALCMs in 270 sorties.

On 11 September 2001 nineteen operatives of Osama bin Laden's al-Qaeda terrorist network launched a co-ordinated and devastating attack on the United States of America. Over 3,100 people lost their lives in the worst terrorist attack in America's history. Within days of the attacks, combat operations in the

◄ ► Redundant B-52s at Davis-Monthan. By the end of 1992, B-52G no longer flew nuclear missions and the first B-52G was scrapped on 17 August 1992. By early May 1994 all had been retired or were to be broken up for scrap. (Tony Thornborough)

Did you know?

Davis-Monthan AFB and the Arizona-based Aerospace Materiel and Reclamation Center (AMARC) is where deactivated B-52s and other military aircraft go to die. Before an aircraft is stored, guns, ejection seat pyrotechnics, classified equipment and other items are removed; the aircraft's fuel system is drained and pumped full of light oil, which is then drained, leaving an oil film to protect the fuel system. Engine intakes and exhausts are covered and any gaps or cracks in the upper surface of the airframe are sealed with paper and tape.

so-called 'war against terror' were mounted against the Taliban regime of Afghanistan and Osama bin Laden's al-Qaeda leadership and training infrastructure in the country.

B-52Hs of 20th Bomb Squadron from Minot AFB and Air Force Reserve Command's 93rd Bomb Squadron from Barksdale AFB (and a number of B-1Bs) deployed to Diego Garcia

◀ B-52H-145-BW 60-0024 *I'll Be Seeing You* of the 416th Bomb Wing. (Author)

▲ B-52H-170-BW
61-0017 *Renegade* of
the 92nd Bomb Wing.
(Author)

as part of Operation ENDURING FREEDOM. There was some 'traditional' B-52 'carpet-bombing' of the Taliban front line north of Kabul, especially as part of 'softening up' before allied ground attacks were made against defended enemy positions. The

B-52G-100-BW 58-0193 *Iron Maiden* of the 416th Bomb Wing with thirteen Gulf War bomb symbols, flying with the 801st Bomb Wing (P) at Morón, Spain. (Author)

B-52Hs were also used as a psychological weapon, dropping leaflet bombs backed up by the threat of carpet bombing attacks. B-52Hs of the 93rd Bomb Squadron, 917th Bomb Wing, dropped over 13 million pounds of ordnance. By 17 December,

➤ B-52H-155-BW
60-0047 *Neanderthal*.

➤➤ B-52G-95-BW
58-0170 *Special Delivery
II* of the 416th Bomb
Wing at Griffiss AFB,
which operated in the
801st Bomb Wing (P) at
Morón AB, Spain, during
the Gulf War and flew
twenty-three missions.
(USAF)

➤ B-52G-110-BW 58-0237 *Blytheville Storm* of the 328th Bomb Squadron, 93rd Bomb Wing, at Castle AFB, California, taking off from RAF Fairford on 19 February 1991 with twenty-four Mk 82 bombs on underwing MERs. During active duty at Fairford in the 806th Bomb Wing (P), this aircraft flew ten bombing missions against targets in DESERT STORM, 6 February–9 March 1991. (Peter E. Davies)

Did you know?

General John C. Meyer led the LINEBACKER operations from his HQ at Offutt AFB in Omaha, Nebraska. From there, targets were chosen and plans drawn up for the direction of attack and the bomb loads to be carried. An 8th Air Force plan for an all-out mass attack on Hanoi by flying crossing 'Basketweave' flight paths and arriving over targets from different directions to swamp the defences was rejected.

➤ M117 750lb bombs on the underwing stores station of B-52G-95-BW 58-0182 *What's Up Doc?* of the 379th Bomb Wing at RAF Fairford at the time of the Gulf War in 1991. Twenty-four M117 bombs could be carried on the two underwing positions fitted with the redundant Hound Dog pylon and multiple ejector racks. (Via Tony Thornborough)

FWD
TO SADDAM
LOVE KIRK
+
Arlene P
FROM LUCY & TODD!
Bend over and meet your maker
PAM &
ROGER
Z STINGIN Skeeter
Special Delivery
The Williams Family
BEFORE FLIGHT
TO THE HEAD
RAGHEAD
FROM, BLAINE
BOBBY

though B-52Hs flew only 10 per cent of the missions (7,100 USAF sorties), they carried more than 70 per cent of the ordnance. The B-52Hs of the 20th EBS had delivered over 3,500 tons of weapons and had flown more than 400 sorties by January 2002. The 28th Air Expeditionary Wing dropped more than 80 per cent of the weapons based on weight during the whole of that operation, 60 per cent of it consisting of Precision

Did you know?

During 1–3 August 1994 two B-52Hs completed a 20,000-mile round-the-world flight for Global Power 94, which set new aviation world records for the longest and second longest jet sorties. It was also the first such mission to include a live weapon drop, the aircrews bombing a target range in Kuwait en route.

◄ Rockwell B-1B Lancer *The Reluctant Dragon* and B-52H-155-BW 60-0052 of the 5th Bomb Wing at Minot AFB at Mildenhall Air Fête, May 1994. (Author)

➤ B-52G-105-BW 58-0216 *Thunder Struck* of the 69th Bomb Squadron, 42nd Bomb Wing, at Loring AFB, which flew twenty-two missions in the Gulf War, 1992. (Tony Thornborough)

➤➤ 2nd Lieutenant Kelly J. Flinn, in 1995, undergoing training in a simulator with an instructor.

Guided Munitions (PGMs). A number of new weapons received their 'baptism of fire' during ENDURING FREEDOM, including the AGM-142 TV-guided missile, which hit targets successfully in Afghanistan, despite relatively few weapons being expended.

In early March 2003 fourteen B-52Hs were deployed to RAF Fairford and another

Did you know?
In mid-1995 2nd Lieutenant Kelly J. Flinn, the first female B-52 pilot in US Air Force history, underwent crew training with the Formal Training Unit at Barksdale before being assigned to the 5th Bomb Wing at Minot AFB, North Dakota.

fourteen B-52Hs at Barksdale went to Diego Garcia to be used as part of the coalition's 'shock and awe' campaign in IRAQI FREEDOM, the Second Gulf War. Additional B-52Hs were deployed to Andersen AFB, Guam. IRAQI FREEDOM began with coalition aircraft conducting strikes to prepare the battlefield. In all, 15,000 PGMs were dropped and

750 cruise missiles were launched. On 21 March the B-52Hs took part in what has been described as the largest CALCM strike in history, launching seventy-six of more than 140 missiles fired. B-52Hs took part in the so-called 'shock and awe' campaign from the first night of the war, initially attacking and eliminating military and air

Did you know?

AMARC was responsible for scrapping about 365 aircraft over a forty-two-month period to comply with the 1991 Strategic Arms Reduction Treaty (START) conditions. START counted 479 B-52s, 228 of which had been removed from service but not yet reduced to scrap under previous SALT reductions. Destruction had to be conducted in the open so Soviet satellites could see and count each bomber.

defence targets in and around Baghdad. The aircraft were subsequently used against deployed Iraqi Army and Republican Guard formations and targets. B-52Hs flew nearly 300 combat sorties over Iraq, each lasting twelve to seventeen hours on airborne alert, close-air support and interdiction operations, dropping 3.2 million pounds of explosives. They also flew psychological missions, dropping 9 million leaflets over the northern half of Iraq. In all, the B-52Hs flew more than 1,600 flying hours and released more than 2,700 individual weapons. On 9 April Baghdad fell and on 16 April 2003 the end of major combat action in Iraq was declared.

Under present plans, the United States Air Force hopes to keep the B-52H in service well into the 2030s – beyond the B-52's eightieth birthday.

◀ *Dressed To Kill* undergoes maintenance in one of the two special hangars at Barksdale AFB, which permit side-by-side maintenance of two B-52Hs simultaneously. (Author)

▲ B-52Hs of the 11th Bomb Squadron, 2nd Bomb Wing, on the ramp at Barksdale in October 2003. (Author)

➤ *Eagle's Wrath III*. (Author)

▶ B-52H-175-BW 61-0029 *SAC Time*. (Author)

▶▶ B-52H-140-BW 60-0019 *Raz'n Hell II* of the 917th Bomb Wing. (Author)

Did you know?

An innovation first introduced on the B-52C was a new paint job. The undersides of the fuselage and wings were painted in gloss white anti-flash paint. This paint was intended to reflect away some of the thermal radiation from a nuclear detonation, making the B-52C less vulnerable to damage caused by the release of its own bomb. National markings and USAF lettering were not applied over the reflective paint. This system came into vogue in 1956 and was applied to most of those aircraft capable of delivering nuclear weapons.

► B-52Hs of the 11th Bomb Squadron at Barksdale in October 2003. (Author)

►► 11 Sep 01-FDNY-*We Remember* of the 917th Bomb Wing at Barksdale. (Author)

Did you know?

In Operation Iʀᴀǫɪ Fʀᴇᴇᴅᴏᴍ, the Second Gulf War in 2003, B-52Hs were used as part of the coalition's 'shock and awe' campaign against Iraq and the conflict saw the first combat use of the Litening II laser designation pod, which enables the B-52H to launch laser-guided munitions and hit targets with extreme accuracy.

➤ View from the pilot's seat of B-52H-150-BW 60-0045 *Cherokee Strip*. (Author)

➤➤ Major David L. Leedom (left) and 1st Lieutenant Jesse A. Hildebrand at the controls of B-52H-150-BW 60-0045 *Cherokee Strip* of the 93rd Bomb Squadron, 917th Wing, Air Force Reserve Command. (Author)

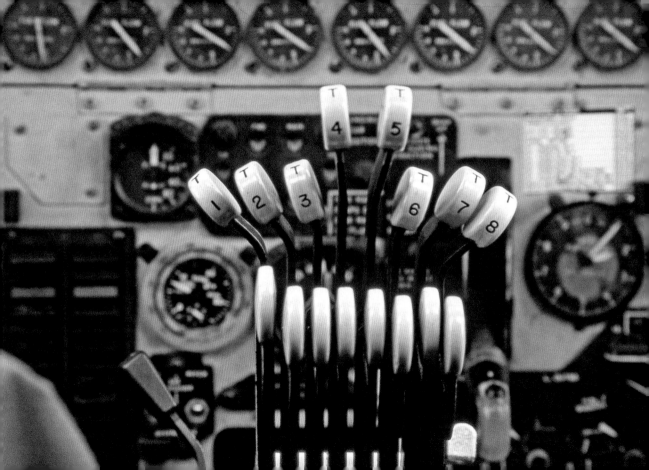

◄ Throttle control levers and the 'crabbing' controls
of a B-52H. (Author)

▲ Coming in to land at Barksdale. (Author)

119

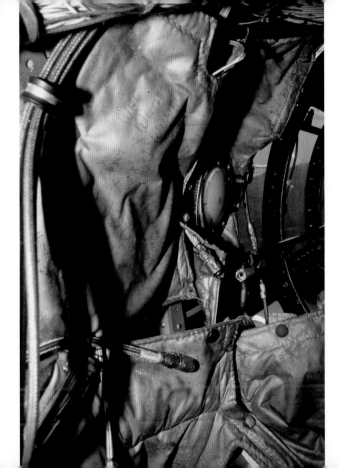

◄◄ B-52H-155-BW 60-0052. (Author)

◄ 'Guam Sucks!' So says graffiti inside the rear fuselage of B-52D-40-BW 56-0689 at the American Air Museum at Duxford, England. (Author)

Did you know?
The B-52H's fatigue life is limited by the life remaining in the upper wing surface. If current attrition and utilisation rates continue, anticipated attrition and fatigue will not bring the B-52H fleet below the sixty-two required until about 2044.

➤ B-52D-40-BW 56-0689 in the American Air Museum at Duxford. This Vietnam veteran was landed there on 8 October 1983 by Lieutenant-Colonel Jim Nerger, who made three circuits before putting the B-52D down over the closed-off M11 motorway. (Author)

Did you know?

The 'Buff' has survived in service into the twenty-first century as a standoff nuclear missile carrier able to operate outside enemy radar detection and then to penetrate at low level and deliver internally carried gravity bombs. Not bad for an aircraft that was first delivered (B-52B) on 29 June 1955!

B-52B

Power plants: Eight Pratt & Whitney J57-P-IWA turbojet engines, each rated at 11,400lb static thrust with water injection

Dimensions: Length: 156ft 6.9in; span: 185ft 0in; height: 48ft 3.6in; wing area: 4,000sq. ft

Weights: Empty: 164,081lb; combat: 272,000lb; maximum take-off: 420,000lb

Armament: Two 20mm M24A1 cannon, with 400 rounds each or four 0.50-calibre M-3 machine guns, with 600 rounds each

Bomb load: About 43,000lb

Performance: Maximum speed at optimum altitude: 546 knots at 19,800ft; service ceiling at combat weight: 47,300ft; combat radius: 3,110 nautical miles

B-52D

Power plants:	Eight Pratt & Whitney J57-P-19W turbojet engines, each rated at 12,100lb static thrust with water injection
Dimensions:	Length: 156ft 6.9in; span: 185ft 0in; height: 48ft 3.6in; wing area: 4,000sq. ft
Weights:	Empty: 177,816lb; combat: 293,100lb; maximum take-off: 450,000lb
Armament:	Four 0.50-calibre M-3 machine guns, with 600 rounds each
Bomb load:	About 60,000lb
Performance:	Maximum speed at optimum altitude: 551 knots at 20,200ft; service ceiling at combat weight: 46,200ft; combat radius: 3,012 nautical miles

B-52G

Power plants:	Eight Pratt & Whitney J57-P-43WB turbojet engines, each rated at 13,750lb static thrust with water injection
Dimensions:	Length: 160ft 10.9in; span: 185ft 0in; height: 40ft 8in; wing area: 4,000sq. ft
Weights:	Empty: 168,445lb; combat: 302,634lb; maximum take-off: 488,000lb
Armament:	Four 0.50-calibre M-3 machine guns with 600 rounds each
Bomb load:	Exceeds 50,000lb
Performance:	Maximum speed at optimum altitude: 551 knots at 20,800ft; service ceiling at combat weight: 47,000ft; combat radius: 3,550 nautical miles

B-52H

Power plants: Eight Pratt & Whitney TF33-P-3 turbofan engines, each rated at 17,000lb static thrust

Dimensions: Length: 156ft 0in; span: 185ft 0in; height: 40ft 8in; wing area: 4,000sq. ft

Weights: Empty: 172,740lb; combat: 306,358lb; maximum take-off: 488,000lb

Armament: One 20mm Vulcan M61 cannon with 1,242 rounds

Bomb load: Over 50,000lb

Performance: Maximum speed at optimum altitude: 547 knots at 23,800ft; service ceiling at combat weight: 47,700ft; combat radius: 4,176 nautical miles

Other titles available in this series

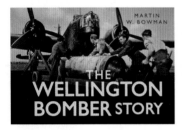

■ ISBN 978 07524 6193-9

■ ISBN 978 07524 6415-2

■ ISBN 978 07524 5080-3

■ ISBN 978 07524 5081-0

■ ISBN 978 07524 5082-7

■ ISBN 978 07524 5303-3